HITS OF THE YEAR

SUR
COUNTY CO

London / New ___ Hong Kong / Tokyo

Published by
Wise Publications
14-15 Berners Street, London W1T 3LJ, UK.

Exclusive Distributors:
Music Sales Limited
Distribution Centre, Newmarket Road,
Bury St Edmunds, Suffolk IP33 3YB, UK.

Music Sales Pty Limited
Units 3-4, 17 Willfox Street, Condell Park, NSW 2200, Australia.

Order No. AM1010262
ISBN: 978-1-78305-876-1
This book © Copyright 2014 Wise Publications,
a division of Music Sales Limited.

Edited by Jenni Norey.
Cover photos:
5 Seconds Of Summer - Astrid Stawiarz/Getty Images –
Taylor Swift - Oliver Hardt/Getty Images –
Meghan Trainor - Bryan Steffy/Getty Images for iHeartMedia –
Pharrell Williams -Larry Busacca/WireImage/Getty Images.

Printed in the EU.

Your Guarantee of Quality
As publishers, we strive to produce every book
to the highest commercial standards.
The music has been freshly engraved and the
book has been carefully designed to minimise
awkward page turns and to make playing from
it a real pleasure.
Particular care has been given to specifying acid-free,
neutral-sized paper made from pulps which have not
been elemental chlorine bleached.
This pulp is from farmed sustainable forests and was
produced with special regard for the environment.
Throughout, the printing and binding have been
planned to ensure a sturdy, attractive publication
which should give years of enjoyment.
If your copy fails to meet our high standards,
please inform us and we will gladly replace it.

www.musicsales.com

ALL ABOUT THAT BASS MEGHAN TRAINOR 4

ALL OF ME JOHN LEGEND 10

BUDAPEST GEORGE EZRA 16

GHOST ELLA HENDERSON 22

HAPPY PHARRELL WILLIAMS 30

I SEE FIRE ED SHEERAN 46

LET IT GO IDINA MENZEL 56

NOBODY TO LOVE SIGMA 64

ONLY LOVE CAN HURT LIKE THIS PALOMA FAITH 39

RATHER BE CLEAN BANDIT FEAT. JESS GLYNNE 68

RUDE MAGIC! 74

SAY SOMETHING A GREAT BIG WORLD FEAT. CHRISTINA AGUILERA 80

SHAKE IT OFF TAYLOR SWIFT 87

SHE LOOKS SO PERFECT 5 SECONDS OF SUMMER 94

SING ED SHEERAN 102

A SKY FULL OF STARS COLDPLAY 128

STAY WITH ME SAM SMITH 110

STEAL MY GIRL ONE DIRECTION 114

SUPERHEROES THE SCRIPT 120

TAKE ME TO CHURCH HOZIER 137

All About That Bass

Words & Music by Kevin Kadish & Meghan Trainor

Yeah, it's pret-ty clear: I ain't no size two. But I can shake it, shake it like I'm sup-posed to do.

'Cause I got that boom boom__ that all the boys chase and all__ the right junk in all__ the right plac-es.

1. I see the ma-ga-zine work-in' that Pho-to - shop.
(2.) boot-y back.__ Go a-head and tell them skin-ny

We know that shit ain't__ real,
bitch-es that.__

come on now, make it stop. If you got beau-ty, beau-ty, just raise 'em up 'cause ev-'ry
No I'm just play-ing. I know you think you're fat.__ But I'm here to tell ya: Ev-'ry

all a-bout that bass, 'bout that bass, no tre-ble. I'm all a-bout that bass, 'bout that bass, no tre-ble. I'm

all a-bout that bass, 'bout that bass, no tre-ble. I'm all a-bout that bass, 'bout that bass.

All Of Me

Words and Music by John Stephens and Toby Gad

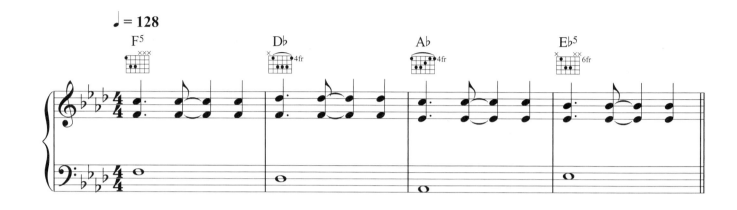

1. What would I do with-out your smart mouth draw-ing me
2. How man-y times do I have to tell you? E - ven when you're

in and you kick-ing me out?____ You got my____ head spin-ning.
cry-ing, you're beau-ti-ful too.____ The world is____ beat-ing____ you

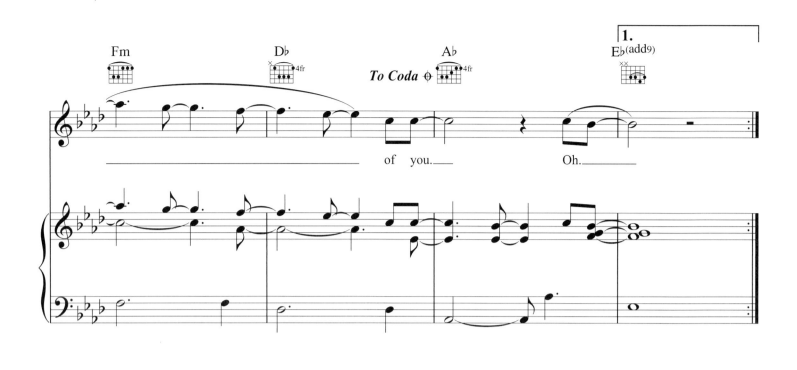

of you.___ Oh._____

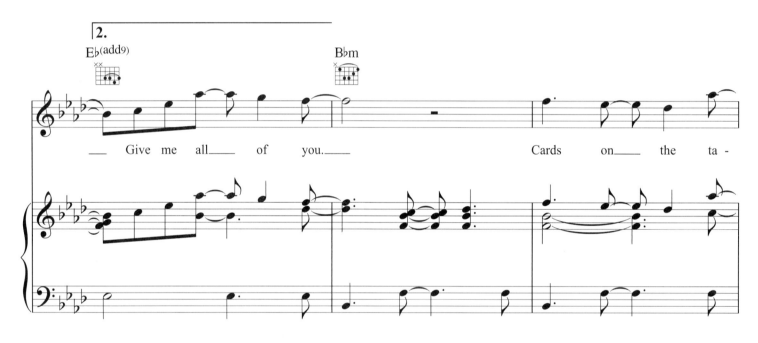

___ Give me all___ of you.___ Cards on___ the ta -

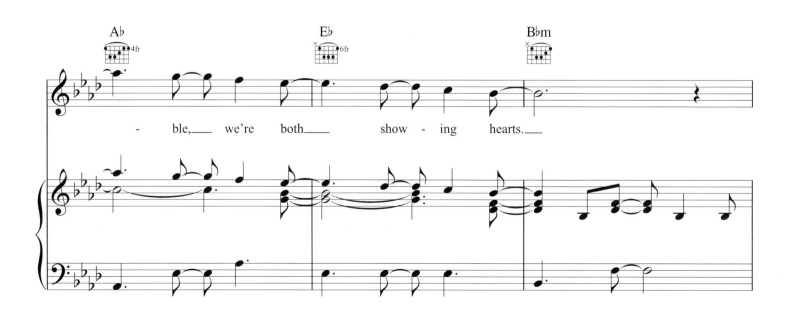

- ble,___ we're both___ show - ing hearts.___

Budapest

Words & Music by George Ezra Barnett & Joel Laslett Pott

1. My house in Bu-da-pest, my,___ my hid-den trea-sure chest.___

Gold-en grand pi-a-no,___ my beau-ti-ful cas-til-lo. You,___ ooh,___

you,   ooh,___ I'd leave it   all.

2. My ac - res of a land,___   I have a-chieved.   It may be hard for you to___
3. My man - y ar - ti - facts,___   the list goes on.   If you just say the words I'll,___
4. My friends and fa - mi - ly, they___   don't un - der- stand.   They fear they'll lose so much if___

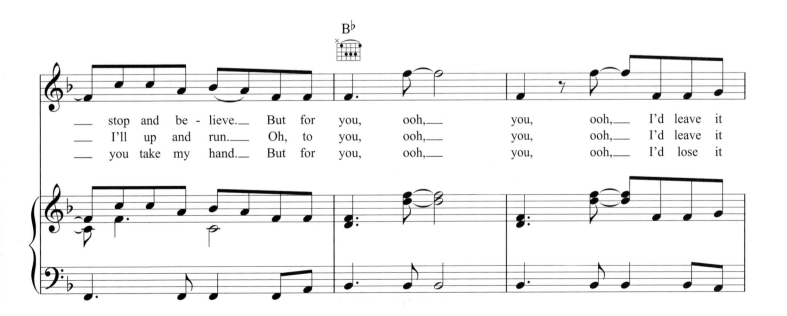

___ stop and be - lieve.___ But for   you,   ooh,___   you,   ooh,___ I'd leave it
___ I'll up and run.___ Oh, to   you,   ooh,___   you,   ooh,___ I'd leave it
___ you take my hand.___ But for   you,   ooh,___   you,   ooh,___ I'd lose it

all.
all.
all.
Oh, for you, ooh,___
Oh, for you, ooh,___
Oh, for you, ooh,___

you, ooh,___ I'd leave it all.
ooh, ooh,___ I'd leave it all.
you, ooh,___ I'd lose it all.

Give me one good rea - son why I___ should nev - er make a change.___

Ba - by, if you hold me then all__

__ of this will go____ a - way.____

Give me one good rea - son why I_____ should nev - er make a change._____

Ba - by, if you hold me then all____ of this will go____ a - way.____

Ah ooh.

Ah

ooh.

Ghost

Words & Music by Ryan Tedder, Noel Zancanella
& Ella Henderson

I keep going to the river to pray ___ 'cause I need something that can wash out the pain. ___ And at most I'm sleeping all these demons away. ___ But your ghost, the ghost of you, it keeps me awake.

Happy

Words & Music by Pharrell Williams

1. It might seem cra - zy what I'm 'bout to say.___

___ Sun - shine,___ she's here,___

___ you can take a break._____ I'm a

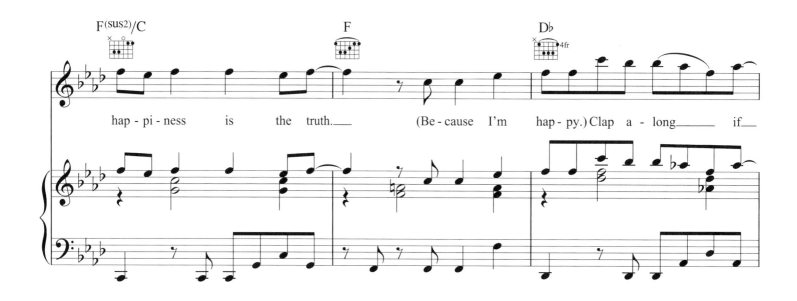

hap - pi - ness is the truth.___ (Be - cause I'm hap - py.) Clap a - long___ if___

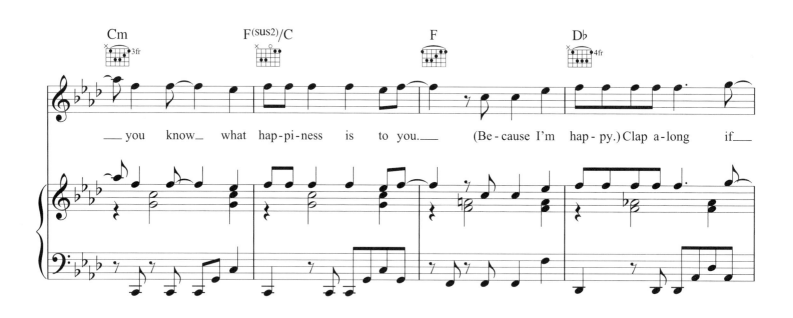

___ you know___ what hap - pi - ness is to you.___ (Be - cause I'm hap - py.) Clap a - long if___

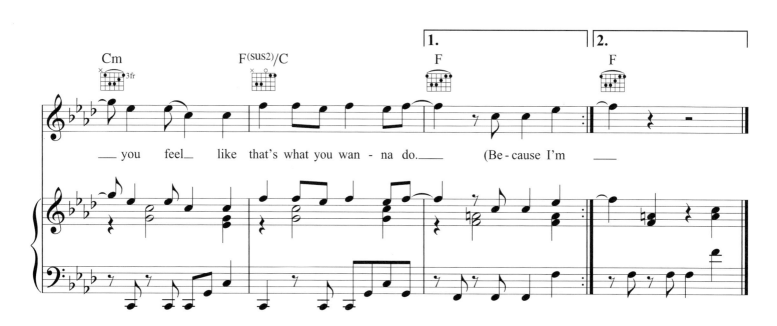

___ you feel___ like that's what you wan - na do.___ (Be - cause I'm ___

Only Love Can Hurt Like This

Words & Music by Diane Warren

got no hold on me._____ But when you're not there   I just crum - ble.
I'm beg-ging you to stay._____ And when you come close   I just trem - ble.

I tell my - self   I don't care that   much,_____   but I feel like   I   die_____
And ev - 'ry__ time,__   ev -'ry time you go_____   it's like__ a   knife_____

till I feel your touch._____   On - ly__ love,_____   on - ly love can hurt like__ this.__
that cuts right__ through my soul.

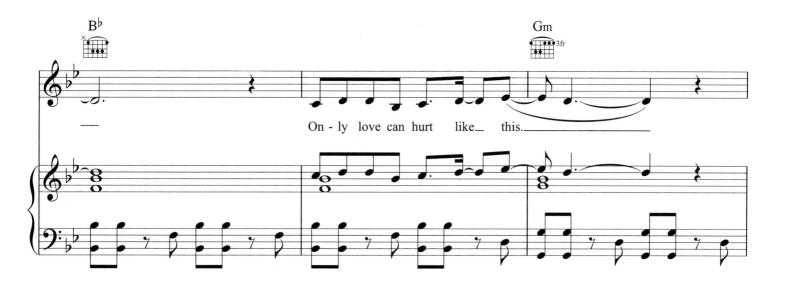

On - ly love can hurt like this.

Must have been a dead-ly kiss, on - ly love can hurt like this.

On - ly love can hurt like this. Your

43

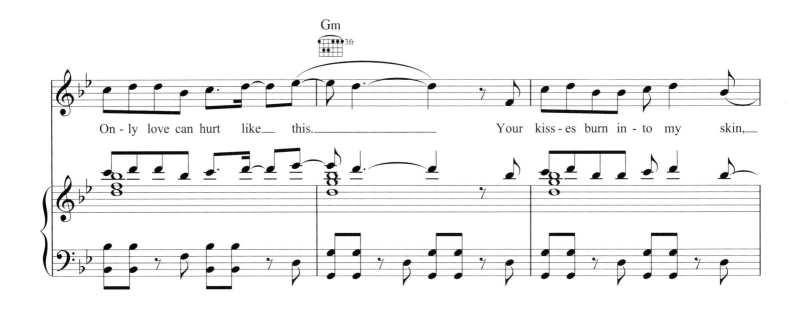

On - ly love can hurt like__ this.__ Your kiss - es burn in - to my skin,__

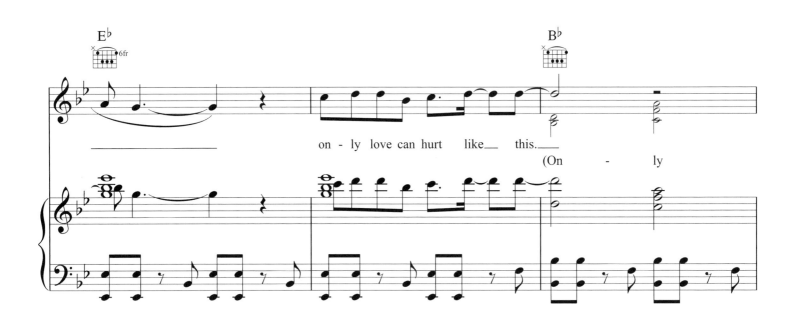

on - ly love can hurt like__ this.__ (On - ly

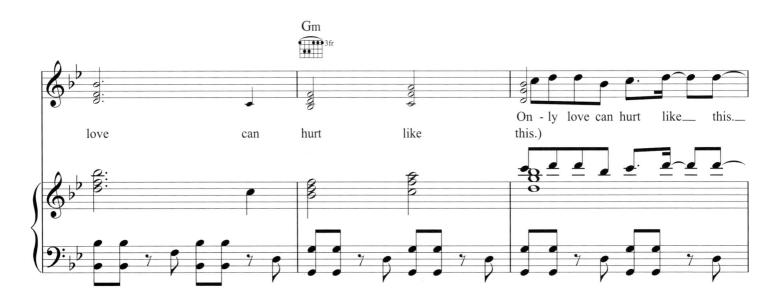

love   can hurt   like   this.)   On - ly love can hurt like__ this.__

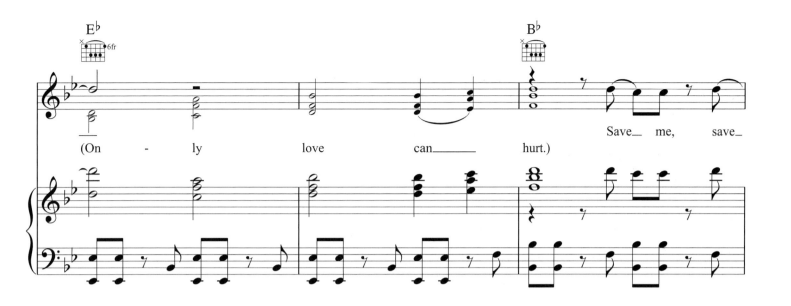

(On - ly love can hurt.) Save__ me, save__

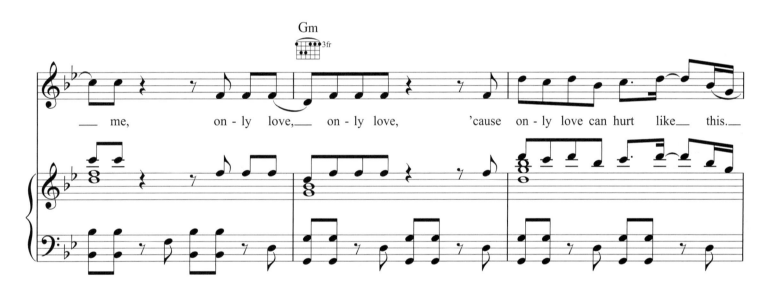

__ me, on - ly love,__ on - ly love, 'cause on - ly love can hurt like__ this.__

And it must have__ been a dead - ly kiss.__

I See Fire

Words & Music by Ed Sheeran

Moderately slow ♩ = 76

Guitar chords with capo, 6th fret

* Melody sung in octaves throughout. †Symbols in parentheses represent chord names with respect to capoed guitar.
Symbols above represent actual sounding chords.

48

Let It Go

Music and lyrics by Kirsten Anderson-Lopez and Robert Lopez

Nobody To Love

Words & Music by Ronnie Self, John Legend, Ernest Wilson, Kanye West,
Mike Dean, Charles Wilson, Bobby Massey, Lester McKenzie, Bobby Dukes,
Che Pope, Malik Jones, Cydel Young, Sakiya Sandifer, Norman Whiteside & Elon Rutberg

leav-ing this par - ty with no - bod-y to love.__ No - bod-y, no-bod-y._____

Rather Be

Words & Music by James Napier, Grace Chatto
& Jack Patterson

D.S. al Coda

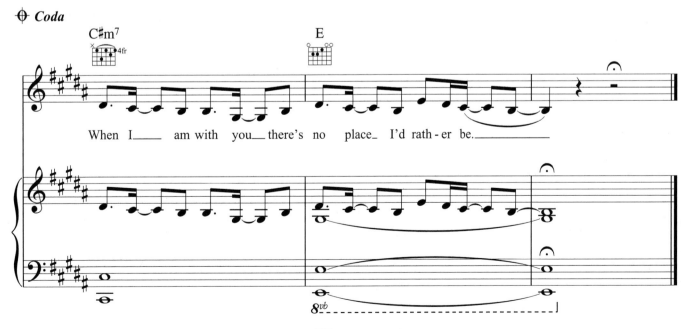

Rude

Words & Music by Nasri Atweh, Adam Messinger,
Ben Spivak, Mark Pellizzer & Alexander Tanasijczuk

we'll be a fam-i-ly.   Why you got-ta be so

rude._____

1.

I hate to do this, you leave no choice,   can't live with - out her.

Love me or hate me, we will be boys,   stand-ing at that al - tar.

77

Or we will run a-way to an-oth-er gal-ax-y.___ You know,

you know she's in love with me. She will go an-y-where I go.

2.

rude.___

Say Something

Words & Music by Mike Campbell, Chad Vaccarino
& Ian Axel

Shake It Off

Words & Music by Max Martin, Taylor Swift
& Shellback

shake, shake, shake.__ I shake it off, I shake it off. (Hoo, hoo,__ hoo!) Heart-

Am
-break-ers gon-na break, break, break, break, break__ and the fak-ers gon-na fake, fake,

C

fake, fake, fake.__ Ba-by, I'm just gon-na shake, shake, shake, shake, shake.__ I

G

1.
shake it off, I shake it off. (Hoo, hoo,__ hoo!)

2, 3.
off. (Hoo, hoo,__ hoo!)
2. I nev-er miss a

dirty cheats in the world you could have been getting down to this sick beat.

My ex - man brought his new girl - friend. She's like "oh my God", but

I'm just gon - na shake. And to the fel - la o - ver there with the hel - la good hair. Won't you

come on o - ver, ba - by, we can shake, shake, shake. Yeah,_____ oh._____

'Cause the

D.S. al Coda

Shake it off, I shake it off, I, I, I shake it off, I shake it

off, I, I, I shake it off, I shake it off, I, I, I

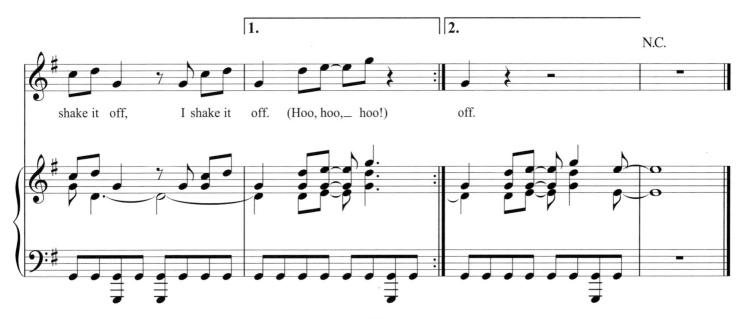

shake it off, I shake it off. (Hoo, hoo,— hoo!) off.

She Looks So Perfect

Words & Music by Michael Clifford, Ashton Irwin
& Jacob Sinclair

98

100

Sing

Words & Music by Pharrell Williams & Ed Sheeran

we could get down, now. I don't wan-na know if you're get-ting a-head of the pro-gram. I want you to be mine, lady, and to hold your bod-y close. Take an-oth-er step in-to the no-man's land, for the long-est time lady. I

need you darl - ing, come on set the tone._ If you feel you're fall - ing, won't you let me know._ Oh, oh,_

ooh._ Oh, oh,_ ooh._

If you love_ me come on get in - volved,_ feel it rush - ing through_ you from your head to toe._ Oh, oh,_

ooh._ Oh, oh,_ ooh._ Sing!

then we got noth-ing to say— and noth-ing to know but some-thing to drink— and may-be some-thing to smoke.—

C#m

Let it go un-til our roles all change,— sing-ing we found love in a lo-cal rave.— No,

I don't real-ly know what I'm sup-posed to say.— But I can just fi-gure it out and hope and pray.— I

G#m

told her my name— and said "It's nice to meet— ya." Then she hand-ed me a bot-tle of wa-ter filled with te-qui-la.

Stay With Me

Words & Music by Tom Petty, Jeff Lynne,
James Napier, Sam Smith & William Phillips

1. Guess it's true I'm not good at a one night stand.
2. Why am I so e - mo - tion - al?

But I still need love 'cause I'm just a man.
No, it's not a good look, gain some self con - trol.

Steal My Girl

Words & Music by Wayne Hector, John Ryan, Julian Bunetta,
Ed Drewett, Liam Payne & Louis Tomlinson

1. She be my queen since we were six-teen. We want the same things. We dream the same dreams, al-right.
2. Kiss-es like cream, her walk is so mean and ev-'ry jaw drop when she's in those jeans, al-right.

(Al-right.)
(Al-right.)

I got it all 'cause she is the one. Her mum calls me 'love', her dad calls me 'son',__ al-right.__
I don't ex-ist if I don't have her. The sun does-n't shine, the world does-n't turn,__ al-right.__

(Al-right.)
(Al-right.)

I know,__

115

Superheroes

Words & Music by Mark Sheehan, Daniel O'Donoghue
& James Barry

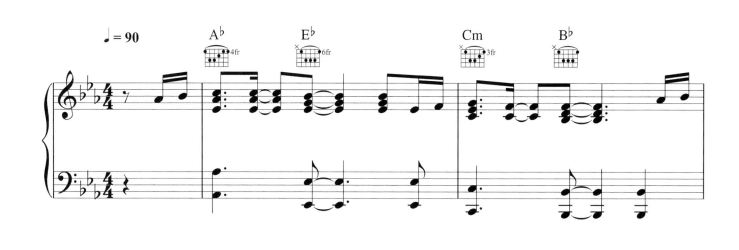

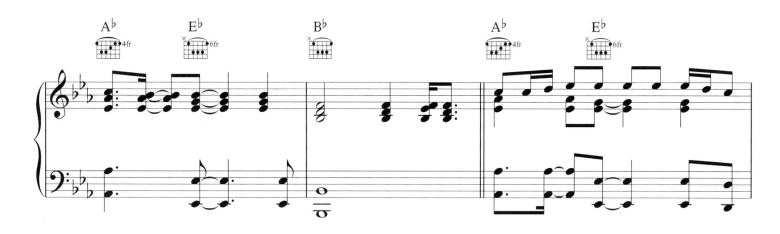

1. All her life_

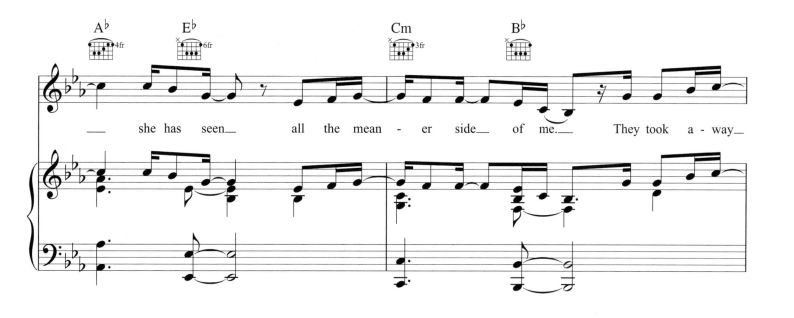

she has seen___ all the mean - er side___ of me.___ They took a - way___

___ the proph-et's dream___ for a prof - it on___ the street.___ Now she's

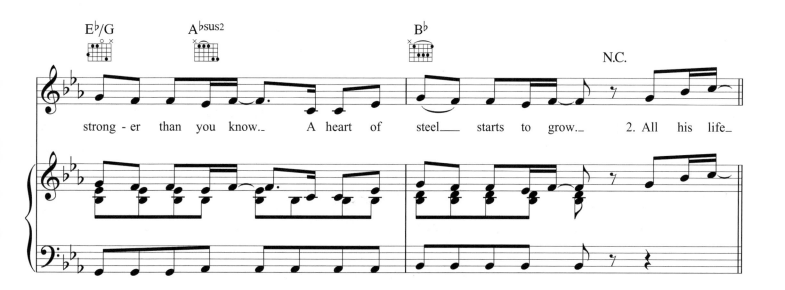

strong - er than you know.___ A heart of steel___ starts to grow.___ 2. All his life___

all your_ life you've been strug-gl-ing to make things_ right, that's how a su-per-he-ro

learns to___ fly._____ Ev-'ry day, ev-'ry ho-ur, turn the pain___ in - to pow-er. When you've been fight-ing for it

all your_ life you've been work-ing ev-'ry day and_ night, that's how a su-per-he-ro

learns to___ fly._____
Ev-'ry day, ev-'ry ho-ur, turn the pain in-to pow-er.

1.
(Oh,   oh, oh,   oh.)   (Oh,   oh, oh,   oh.)
3. All the

2, 3.
Pow-er,   pow-er,   pow-er,   pow-er.

Pow-er,   pow-er,   pow-er,   pow-er. Ev-'ry

day, ev-'ry ho-ur, turn the pain in-to pow-er. Pow-er, pow-er, pow-er, pow-er.

Pow-er, pow-er, pow-er, pow-er. Ev-'ry

She's got lions in her heart, a fi-re in her soul. He's got a

day, ev-'ry ho-ur, turn the pain in-to pow-er.

A Sky Full Of Stars

Words & Music by Guy Berryman, Jonathan Buckland,
William Champion, Christopher Martin & Tim Bergling

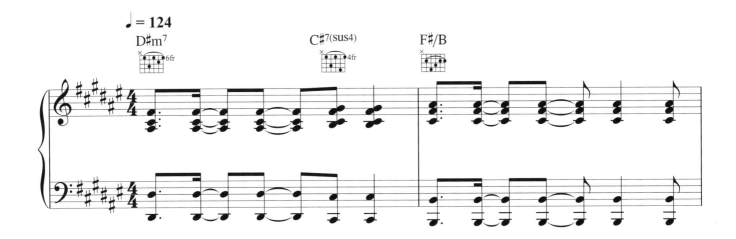

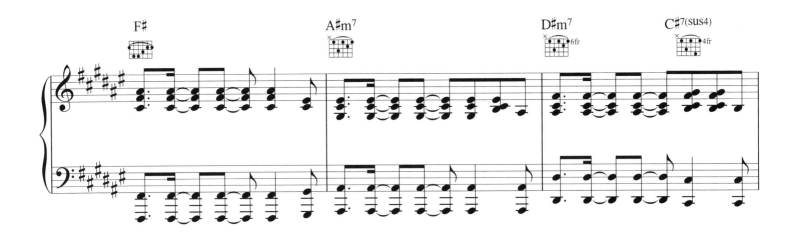

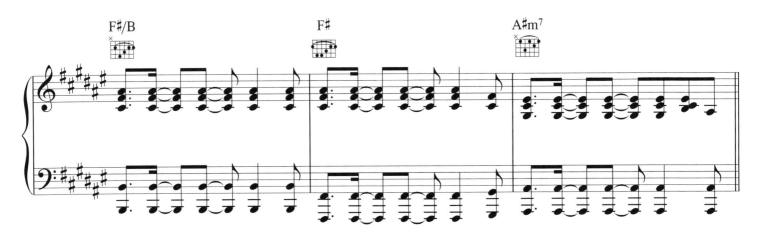

1. 'Cause you're a sky,_____ 'cause you're a sky_____ full of stars._
2. 'Cause you're a sky,_____ 'cause you're a sky_____ full of stars._

I'm gon-na give_____ you my heart._
I wan-na die_____ in your arms._

'Cause you're a
'Cause you get

sky,_____'cause you're a sky_____ full of stars.____
light - er the more_____ it gets dark.____

'Cause you light_____ up the path.____ }
I'm gon - na give_____ you my heart.____ }

And I don't care,_____ go on and

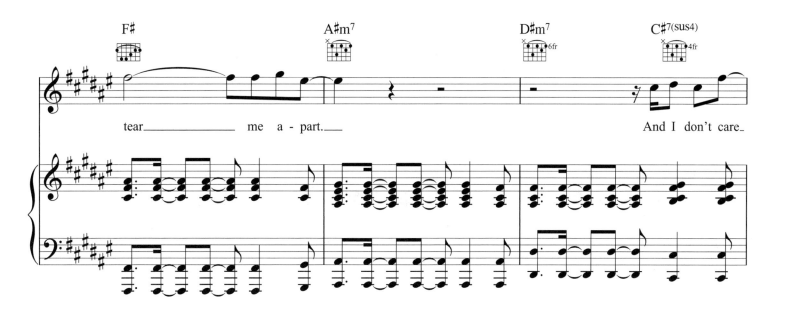

tear_____ me a - part.____   And I don't care_

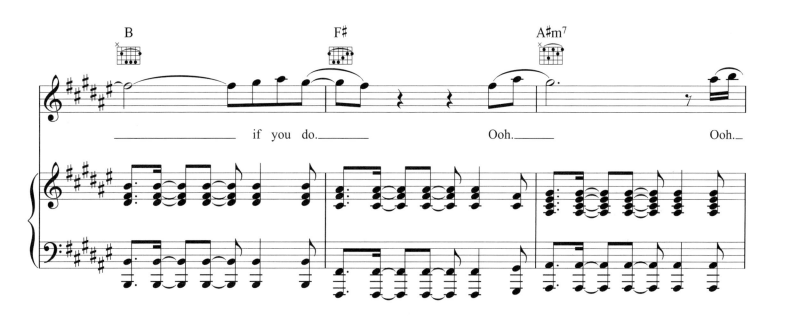

_____ if you do._____   Ooh._____   Ooh._

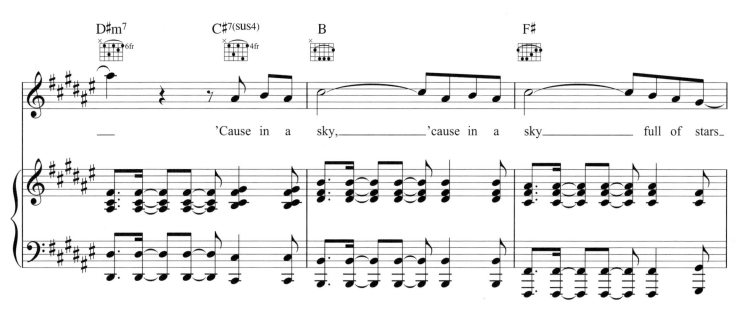

___   'Cause in a sky,_____ 'cause in a sky_____ full of stars_

I think I saw   you._____

2º see

To Coda ⊕

I think I see you.

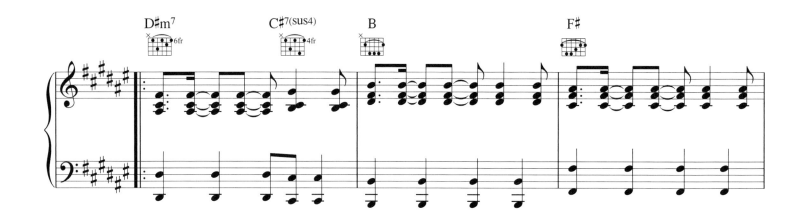

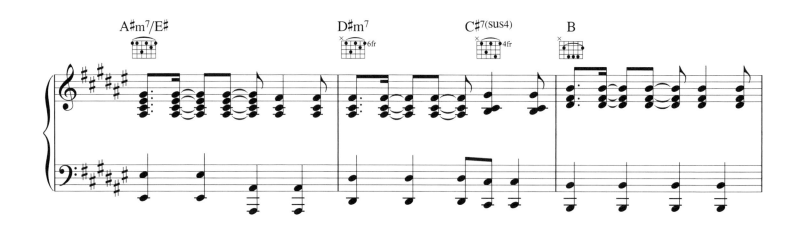

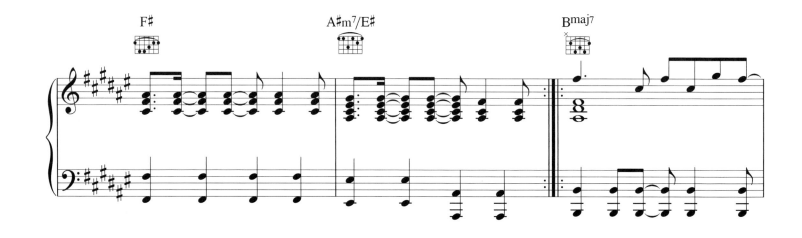

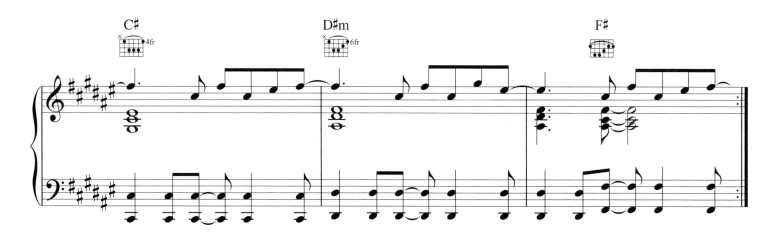

'Cause you're a sky,___ you're a sky___ full of stars.___

___ Such a heav-en-ly view.___

___ You're such a heav-en-ly view.___

135

(Ooh._____

Ooh.)

136

Take Me To Church

Words & Music by Andrew Hozier-Byrne

23456789